An Understandable Guide to Music Theory

The Most Useful Aspects of Theory for Rock, Jazz & Blues Musicians

(3rd Edition)

by Chaz Bufe

See Sharp Press • Tucson, Arizona • 1994

For information write to See Sharp Press, P.O. Box 1731,
Tucson, Arizona 85702-1731.
Web site: www.seesharppress.com

Bufe, Charles.
    An understandable guide to music theory / by Charles
Bufe. – 3rd ed. – Tucson, AZ : See Sharp Press, 1994.
    80 pp. : music ; 28 cm.
    Includes bibliographical references. (p. 74)
    ISBN 1-884365-00-0 (pbk.)

    1. Music – Theory.   I. Title.

          780.1

Third Edition
        First Printing—June 1994
        Second Printing—October 1996
        Third Printing—July 1999
        Fourth Printing—September 2001
        Fifth Printing—September 2005

Cover and interior design by Charles Bufe. Cover graphics
© Clifford Harper. Interior set in Times Roman and Helvetica,
cover typeset in Friz Quadrata. Printed on acid-free paper with
soy-based ink by Thomson-Shore, Inc., Dexter, Michigan.

Contents

V. Form

VI. Useful Techniques

VII. Instrumentation

Introduction

Music theory is a broad field. It covers many topics—melody, rhythm, form, harmony, orchestration, and counterpoint—on which thousands of works have been written; and it can appear very intimidating. But it needn't be, and in fact it can be a great help to musicians playing almost any type of music.

An Understandable Guide to Music Theory is a "user's manual" which concentrates on those aspects of theory that are of most practical use to people playing and writing music, be it rock, jazz, blues, reggae, or salsa. To help make this information easy to understand, I've included over 100 musical examples, and I've avoided the use of technical language where possible. In the few places where I couldn't avoid using technical terms, I've thoroughly explained them. So, any musician who can read music should easily comprehend the material contained in this book.

Some may ask, "why study theory?" The answer is that music theory is a valuable set of tools, and it's self-defeating to attempt to build anything—be it a house, a song, or a symphony—unless you're thoroughly familiar with the tools you're using to construct it. And an understanding of music theory will give you the tools you need to expand your musical horizons; it'll give you the tools you need to make the kind of music that you want.

—Chaz Bufe, May 20, 1994

Scales

All scales and chords are simply patterns of intervals, and intervals are simply the distances between notes. They are measured in "steps." The distance between adjacent white and black keys on the piano, or adjacent frets on the guitar, is one half-step. The distance between two white keys separated by a black key, or two frets separated by another, is a whole step. All intervals have names corresponding to the distance between the notes in them.

Table 1

Distance Between Notes	Interval	Abbreviation
1/2 step	minor 2nd (semitone)	m2
1 step	Major 2nd (whole tone)	M2
11/2 steps	minor 3rd (Augmented 2nd)	m3, A2
2 steps	Major 3rd	M3
21/2 steps	Perfect 4th	P4
3 steps	Augmented 4th, diminished 5th (tritone)	A4, d5
31/2 steps	Perfect 5th	P5
4 steps	minor 6th (Augmented 5th)	m6, A5
41/2 steps	Major 6th	M6
5 steps	minor 7th (Augmented 6th)	m7, A6
51/2 steps	Major 7th	M7
6 steps	Octave	8ve

The following musical example shows intervals as distances from middle C to notes above it, and between notes selected at random.

Example 1

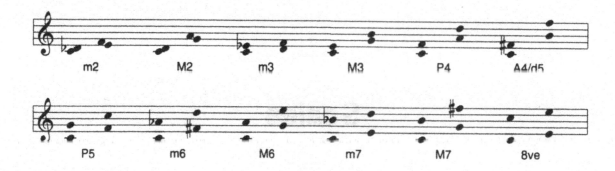

The names for intervals wider than an octave are found by moving the upper note down an octave and adding the resultant interval to the number seven (*not* eight). For example, the interval from middle C to Db above high C would be a minor 9th (7 plus a minor 2nd).

Example 2

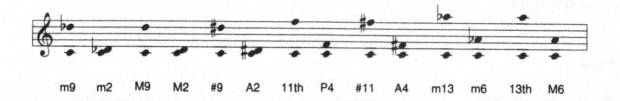

These are the only intervals normally referred to in the octave-plus range; the other notes above an octave—10th, 12th, and 14th—duplicate notes already present as the 3rd, 5th, or 7th in most chords with members (notes) more than an octave above their roots. It's also worth noting that there is more than one way to refer to many of these intervals. Beyond the octave, it's probably more common to refer to intervals containing sharped or flatted notes as "sharp" or "flat" rather than "augmented" or "minor." So, for example, a flat 9th (or ♭9, or flatted 9th) is the same as a minor 9th, and a sharp 9th (or ♯9) is the same as an augmented 9th.

Don't be frightened by all of these intervals; their names are simply a convenient form of musical shorthand which musicians use to make communicating with each other easier. If you spend much time with other musicians, you'll get used to hearing and using these interval names in short order.

Major Scales

The most familiar scale is the major scale, do-re-mi-fa-sol-la-ti-do. The easiest way to the think of the major scale (C major in this case) is as the white keys of the piano, with the scale beginning and ending on C.

The distances between the notes in the C major scale are not equal. The notes E and F (the third and fourth degrees—notes—of the scale) and B and C (seventh and first degrees) are adjacent on the piano, while all of the other notes in the scale have a black key between them. The distance from E to F and from B to C is a half-step, or minor 2nd; the distance between the other notes in the scale is a whole step, or major 2nd.

Example 3

All other major scales have the same arrangement of whole steps and half-steps as the C major scale. Here are two examples, the D major and E♭ major scales:

Example 4

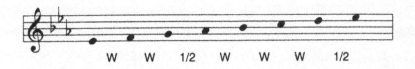

At this point you might be wondering how you can figure out where the major scale starts in various key signatures. The easiest way in sharp key signatures is to remember that the major scale starts a half-step above the last sharp (the sharp farthest to the right). So, for example, when the last sharp is C♯, the key is D major, and when the last sharp is G♯, the key is A major.

Example 5

D major (last sharp is C sharp)

A major (last sharp is G sharp)

The procedure is almost as simple with flat key signatures. When only one flat is present in the key signature, that key signature is F major—in other words, the major scale begins and ends on F. When more than one flat is present, the key signature is that of the next-to-the-last flat to the right. So, for example, when the next-to-the-last flat is E♭, the key is E♭ major, and when the next-to-the-last flat is D♭, the key is D♭ major.

Example 6

F major (one flat)

Eb major (next-to-last flat is E flat)

And, of course, when no flats or sharps are present, the key is C major.

Minor Scales

After the major scale, the next most common type of scale is the minor scale. There are three common forms of the minor scale. The simplest is the *natural* minor, which uses the same notes as the major scale, but which begins and ends on a different note—the sixth note of the major scale.

Example 7

C major   A natural minor

The notes and key signatures of C major and A minor are identical. The only difference is that the minor scale starts on the sixth note of the major scale. Scales sharing the same notes and key signatures are called *relatives*. A minor is the relative minor of C major, and C major is the relative major of A minor. (Scales beginning on the same note, but sharing neither the same key signature nor all of the same notes, are called *parallel*; for example, C minor is the parallel minor of C major.)

The two other common forms of the minor scale—both of which, like the natural minor, begin on the sixth note of the relative major scale—are the *harmonic* and *melodic* minor. The only difference between the natural and the harmonic minor scales is that the seventh note of the harmonic minor is raised half a step above the seventh note of the natural minor, creating a 1½-step (augmented 2nd) gap between the sixth and seventh notes in the scale. So, for example, the notes in the A harmonic minor scale are the same as the notes in the A natural minor except that the seventh note in the harmonic minor scale is a G♯ rather than a G♮ (G natural); and the distance from F (the sixth note in the scale) to G♯ is 1½ steps (an augmented 2nd).

The only difference between the natural minor and the melodic minor scales is that the sixth and seventh notes of the melodic minor are raised half a step above those of the natural minor when ascending; when descending, the notes of the melodic minor are the same as those of the natural minor. For example, the only difference between A natural minor and A melodic minor are that when ascending the sixth and seventh notes of the melodic minor are F♯ and G♯ rather than F and G natural as in the natural minor. (When descending, the two scales are identical.) The following example shows the differences between the G natural, harmonic, and melodic minor scales:

Example 8

G natural minor   G harmonic minor

G melodic minor

The harmonic and melodic minor scales are variations of the natural minor scale—and they're variations with purpose. The melodic minor is more useful for writing and playing melodies, and the harmonic minor is more useful for harmonizing melodies, than the natural minor. (The harmonic minor can, however, be used to good effect melodically, a good example being "Song for the Pharoah Kings" on Chick Corea's *Where Have I Known You Before?* album.) But the natural minor remains a useful scale, and will tend to sound fresh in solos because it's heard less frequently than many other scales.

Modal Scales

Modal scales are relatives of the major scale—scales like the natural minor which utilize the notes and key signature of a major scale, but which begin and end on different notes, and thus have different sequences of intervals. This is most easily seen with the C major scale and its relative modal scales:

Example 9

One method of finding the notes in modal scales is to take the whole step/half-step patterns from example 9 and transpose them. For example, to find the notes in the G Dorian scale, begin the scale on G and follow the whole step/half-step pattern for the Dorian mode:

Example 10

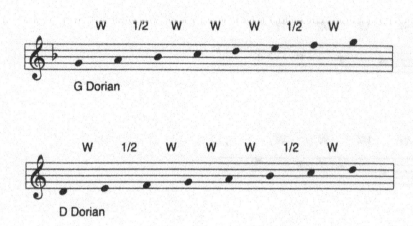

Similarly, to find the notes in A Lydian, you would transpose the Lydian pattern.

Example 11

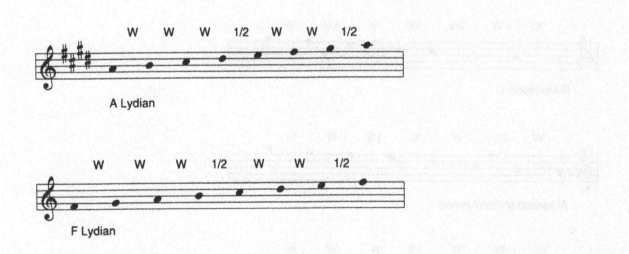

Another way to find the notes in modal scales is to remember that modal scales always use the notes of the major scale and that they always begin on certain notes (degrees) of the major scale. Those notes are:

Table 2

Beginning Note in Major Scale	Mode
1st	Ionian (major)
2nd	Dorian
3rd	Phrygian
4th	Lydian
5th	Mixolydian
6th	Aeolian (natural minor)
7th	Locrian

So, to find the notes in the A Dorian scale, for instance, all you need to do is to find the major scale in which A is the second note (G major).

Example 12

A Dorian (key signature of G major)

And to find the notes in a B♭ Phrygian scale, you need to find the major scale in which B♭ is the third note (G♭ major).

Example 13

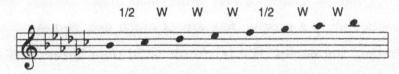

Bb Phrygian (key signature of Gb major)

All of the modes contain certain notes which give them their particular characters, which distinguish them from the major and minor scales and from each other. Those notes are:

Table 3

Mode	Characteristic Note(s)
Dorian	6th
Phrygian	2nd
Lydian	4th
Mixolydian	7th
Locrian	2nd & 5th

In modal melodies, these characteristic notes should be emphasized in order to retain the modal flavor. We're so used to hearing the major and minor scales that our ears, given half a chance, will hear modal melodies as being major or minor; to avoid this, it's necessary to emphasize the characteristic notes of the modes. Similarly, when harmonizing modal melodies, the most important chords are the chord rooted on the first note of the scale and chords containing the characteristic note(s).

It's worth noting that the Locrian mode is rarely used and can for all practical purposes be ignored. The reason for this is that its first and fifth notes form a tritone, which has a very strong tendency to resolve to the relative major, which would destroy the modal feeling. For instance, the B Locrian mode has a strong tendency to resolve to C major. So, it's very tricky to use the Locrian mode effectively. As well, there's little point in using this mode, as the Phrygian mode, which also has the flatted 2nd as a characteristic note, can often be used in place of the much harder-to-use Locrian.

Synthetic Scales

The theoretical number of synthetic scales—scales other than major, minor, and modal—is astronomical. In practice, only a relative few are of much use, and most of them are scales from which "tertian" harmonies (that is, chords build from intervals of a third—major, minor, 7th, and 9th chords, for example) can be constructed.

Synthetic scales can be classified in several ways. The simplest is to divide them into two types: asymmetric and symmetric. The most common of the useful synthetic scales are asymmetric. The most familiar of these is the diatonic pentatonic (five-note) scale. (While there are other pentatonic scales, the diatonic pentatonic is by far the most common; references to the "pentatonic scale" almost always refer to the diatonic pentatonic.) This scale is very useful to beginning improvisers, in that it's virtually impossible to make a mistake when using it. There are actually five versions of the pentatonic scale, each utilizing the same notes, but beginning on a different note:

Example 14

There are other types of pentatonic scale; three of the most common are:

Example 15

Another very familiar asymmetric scale is the blues scale. It's a wonderful tool, but it's overworked. When you use the blues scale, it's usually a good idea to mix it in with other scales. (Notice the similarity between the C blues scale and the fifth version of the Eb diatonic pentatonic—of which C is the relative minor.)

Example 16

C blues scale   Eb pentatonic (fifth version)

The Hungarian minor is another useful asymmetric scale. Like the pentatonic scales with flatted third notes, it can be used to produce "oriental"-sounding melodies. The Hungarian minor is, however, especially well suited to producing such melodies because it contains *two* augmented 2nd (1½-step) intervals, which are characteristic of "oriental" melodies.

Example 17

Hungarian Minor

While the preceding scales are the most commonly encountered asymmetric synthetic scales, there are many other useful asymmetric scales. The following example features several which you might find of use:

Example 18

Overtone

Overtone Blues

Spanish Phrygian

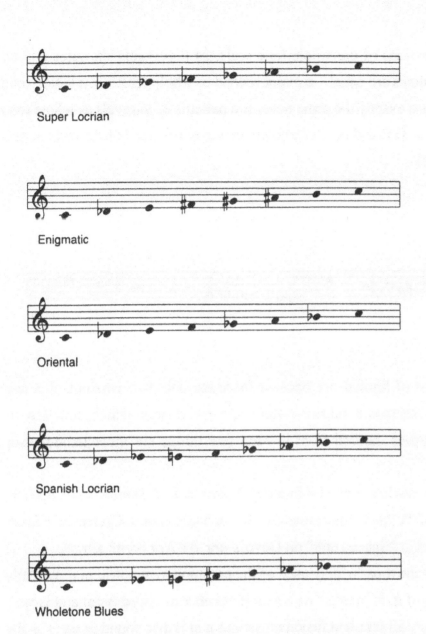

Super Locrian

Enigmatic

Oriental

Spanish Locrian

Wholetone Blues

Symmetric synthetic scales—scales with regularly repeating patterns of intervals within an octave—are less common, but are very useful. A distinguishing feature of all such scales is that they come in either one, two, three, four, or six versions. (Major, minor, modal, and asymmetric synthetic scales all come in twelve versions—versions starting on C, C♯, D, D♯, etc.) Because of the regularly repeating patterns within them, versions of the same symmetric scale beginning on different notes will contain both the same notes and the same pattern of intervals. That can easily be shown with the whole tone scale.

There are only two versions of the whole tone scale, as it contains six notes and all intervals between adjacent notes are equal—a major second or whole tone. So, a whole tone scale beginning on C contains exactly the same notes and patterns of intervals as whole tone scales beginning on D, E, F♯, G♯, and A♯. The other version of the whole tone scale begins on D♭ (or E♭, F, G, A, or B).

Example 19

Whole Tone Scale

The whole tone scale is of limited use because there are only two versions of it and because it never resolves harmonic tension—there are no chords which function as dominants (Vs) in progressions derived from it—and few things are more tedious than unresolved tension.

Examples of whole tone scale use can be found in *Voiles* and *Le Tombeau des Naides*, by Debussy; in the bridge of "Vital Transformation" on the Mahavishnu Orchestra's *Inner Mounting Flame* album; and in "Space Junk" on Devo's *Are We Not Men?* album.

The diminished scale is the most widely used of the common symmetric scales. While there are only three versions of it, it "works" with a large number of chord types and is very versatile. It is used by virtually all jazz and fusion musicians and is also found as early as the late 19th century in the works of Rimsky-Korsakov.

Example 20

Diminished Scale

The augmented scale is the least used of the common symmetric scales. There are only four version of it and it "works" with relatively few chords, but even given its limitations this scale is rarely encountered. For an example of its use, see movement IV of Bartok's *Concerto for Orchestra*.

Example 21

Augmented Scale

The other commonly used symmetric scale is the chromatic scale, which is typically employed as a "filler" in runs. Since it contains all 12 notes, there is only one version of the chromatic scale, and it can be used with *any* type of chord.

Example 22

Chromatic Scale

There are many other useful synthetic scales—and you can invent your own. An easy way to do that is to alter a note in, and/or add a note to, a common scale, as in the following example which utilizes the whole tone scale.

Example 23

added note altered note added note

An outstanding example of what can be done with roll-your-own synthetic scales is the work of the brilliant 20th Century French composer and theoretician Olivier Messiaen, who catalogued and made extensive use of symmetric scales containing six or more notes. Two of Messiaen's scales (he refers to them as "modes") are the familiar whole tone and diminished scales. The others are of his own invention.

Messiaen also did some very interesting things with rhythms, and he set forth his theories in an easily understandable book, *The Technique of My Musical Language*. Messiaen's "modes" (neglecting the whole tone and diminished scales) are:

Example 24

12-Tone Rows

Another useful synthetic "scale" is the 12-tone row, which was invented by the Austrian theorist/composer Arnold Schoenberg shortly after World War I. Twelve-tone rows consist of the 12 tones of the chromatic scale arranged in an order determined by the composer. In standard 12-tone practice, none of the notes in a row may be repeated until all of the other notes have sounded.

The number of possible rows is virtually infinite; and there are 48 versions of most rows—that is, there are normally 48 possible versions of the pattern of intervals comprising the row. (Rows can be designed so that there are fewer versions.) Rows can be transposed to start on any note, played backwards (retrograde), upside down (inversion), and backwards and upside down (retrograde inversion).

Example 25

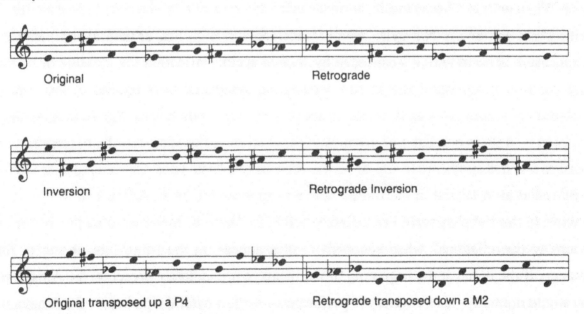

Original   Retrograde

Inversion   Retrograde Inversion

Original transposed up a P4   Retrograde transposed down a M2

Despite their almost limitless numbers, the usefulness of 12-tone rows is rather limited in that their ability to convey emotions is severely restricted. The only moods they really convey well are tension, terror, anguish, suspense, and uncertainty.

Interesting variants of the 12-tone row are 9-, 10-, and 11-note rows. These can be used in the same manner as 12-tone rows, but, in addition, can be used as preparation for passages featuring the tone(s) not in the row(s). After a passage featuring a 9-, 10-, or 11-

note row, a strong entrance highlighting the note(s) omitted in the row can be extremely effective. Consider the following example which uses a 9-note row derived from the 12-note row in the preceding example:

Example 26

Note: When writing 12-tone music, or music using any type of row, the conventions of music writing vary somewhat. Normally, when an accidental (sharp, flat, or natural sign) appears in a measure, it holds until it's cancelled by another accidental within the measure or by the next bar line to the right. But in row writing, an accidental only applies to the note it immediately precedes—that is, all notes are played as naturals unless they're immediately preceded by a sharp or a flat. For instance, if you had an A flat appear at the beginning of a measure and had another note appear on the A space two beats later, that second note would be played as an A natural; if the second note was supposed to be an A flat, you would have to write in the flat sign again immediately before it. There is, however, also the matter of "courtesy cancellations" when successive notes appear on the same line or space: for instance, if the A flat at the beginning of the measure immediately preceded the A natural, you would normally—as a courtesy to performers—write a natural sign before the A natural.

2

Chords

Chords are normally built from scales, and the method used to build chords from major, minor, and modal scales is quite simple. With these scales, you begin on any given note and add every other note above it in the scale. This will give you tertian harmonies—chords built from the interval of a third. Triads, the most basic type of chord, are made up of three notes: a root, and the notes a third and a fifth above it in the scale. Using this every-other-note process you can, for example, construct the following triads from the C major scale:

Example 27

C major   CM   Dm   Em   FM   GM   Am   B dim   CM

The names for the chords starting on each degree (note) of the scale are: 1st–tonic; 2nd–supertonic; 3rd–mediant; 4th–subdominant; 5th–dominant; 6th–submediant; 7th–leading tone. Here, these names correspond to the C major triad (tonic), D minor triad (supertonic), E minor triad (mediant), etc.

The process can be continued. Adding a fourth note creates seventh chords:

Example 28

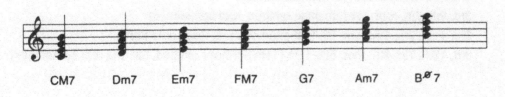

CM7   Dm7   Em7   FM7   G7   Am7   B⌀7

Adding a fifth note creates ninth chords:

Example 29

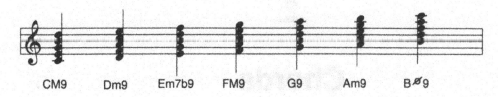

CM9   Dm9   Em7b9   FM9   G9   Am9   B⌀9

Adding a sixth note creates eleventh chords:

Example 30

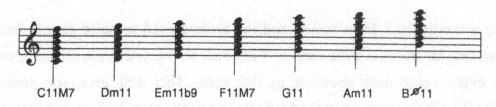

C11M7   Dm11   Em11b9   F11M7   G11   Am11   B⌀11

And adding a seventh note creates thirteenth chords:

Example 31

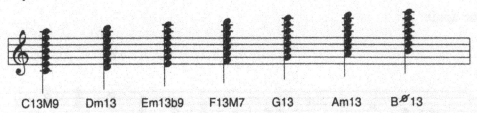

C13M9   Dm13   Em13b9   F13M7   G13   Am13   B⌀13

But that's as far as the process of adding alternate notes in a scale will take you. If you continue the process, you'll duplicate notes already sounded.

When playing multi-note chords, notes are often omitted. The following table lists chord types and the most important notes in them.

Table 4

Chord Type	Essential Notes—*in order of importance*
Triad	root, 3rd, 5th (5th occasionally omitted)
7th	3rd, 7th, root, 5th (5th sometimes omitted)
9th	3rd, 9th, 7th, root, 5th (5th often omitted, root sometimes)
11th	3rd, 11th, 7th, 9th, root, 5th (5th often omitted, root sometimes)
13th	3rd, 13th, 7th, 9th, root, 5th, 11th (11th normally omitted, 5th and root sometimes)

<u>Note</u>: In chords with altered notes (♭5, ♯9, etc.), the altered notes are always sounded.

There is a type of chord which omits the 7th, but which contains additional tones beyond the triad. Such chords are called *added-note* chords. They serve no harmonic function beyond that of the triad; they simply thicken the harmonic texture—they serve as color chords. The three most common added-note chords are the "6th" chord (actually an inversion of a 7th chord—see "Inversions" on p. 23), the "6/9" chord (actually an inversion of an 11th chord), and the added-9th chord.

Example 32

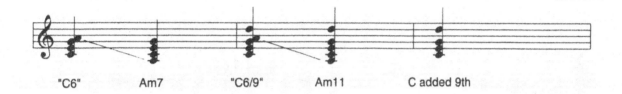

"C6"   Am7   "C6/9"   Am11   C added 9th

Another type of color chord is the chord with an altered note (moved up or down half a step). The most common types are the 7♭5, 7♯5, 7♭9, 7♯9, and ♯11 chords. Altered notes normally resolve (go to notes in the next chord) by moving up or down a step or half step.

Example 33

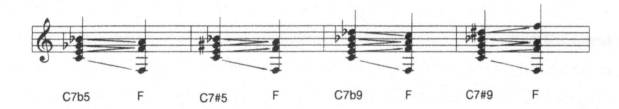

C7♭5   F   C7♯5   F   C7♭9   F   C7♯9   F

<u>Note</u>: References to 7th, 9th, 11th, and 13th chords almost always refer to dominant 7th-(V7) type chords. For instance, an A9 chord would consist of an A7 chord (A, C♯, E, G) plus the 9th (B). Almost invariably, if a writer or composer is referring to a nondominant 7th-type chord, s/he will make note of it. For instance, if a writer refers to an A7 chord, you can be sure that s/he means a dominant-7th type chord, as spelled out above. If that same writer refers to an A minor 7th chord, for example, s/he will either spell it out or use the chord symbol Am7 or, less commonly, A-7. (See Example 43 for a listing of the common chord symbols.)

The process of taking every other note in a scale to produce chords works well with major, minor, and modal scales—but not with synthetic scales. When using synthetic scales, the general practice is to pick the notes in them which produce chords in thirds, the types of chords derived from major, minor and modal scales by taking every other note. The following example shows the chords that can be built from some common synthetic scales. (Altered-note chords are included in the example because, although you can't derive them from major, minor, or modal scales by taking every other note, they are built from intervals of a third.)

Example 34

Diminished Scale

Augmented Scale

Whole Tone Scale

Of course, it's also possible to build chords in fourths from certain synthetic scales (though not from the scales displayed on this page). Messiaen's "modes" (see p. 16), among other synthetic scales, lend themselves to construction of chords in fourths. (See also "Chords in 4ths" on page 24.)

Inversions

Chords do not always appear in root position (with the root in the bass); instead, they often appear in inversions, that is, with notes other than the root in the bass. To find the root in inverted chords, rearrange the notes until you come up with a chord built from thirds—the lowest note in it will be the root. An easy way to do that is to move the top note down an octave whenever you find an even-numbered (2nd, 4th, 6th) interval in a chord. The intervals between the notes in tertian harmonies (chords built from thirds) will all be odd-numbered when the chords are in root position.

Example 35

Root   1st   2nd   3rd

C7 in root position and inversions

The Overtone Series

Chords are not always built from thirds, although chords in thirds are the most natural because they're based on the overtone series. When you pluck a guitar string, for instance, you produce tones at several different frequencies, with the lowest being the loudest. The tones above it will be multiples of the frequency—the number of vibrations per second—of the lowest tone (the fundamental). If the lowest tone has a frequency of 100 cycles per second, the tones above it, its harmonics or overtones, will be at 200, 300, 400, etc. cycles per second, and the 200-cycle tone (second harmonic) will be an octave above the fundamental, the 300-cycle tone (third harmonic) will be an octave and a fifth above the fundamental, etc. (See Example 36.) The overtones are not heard separately, but instead combine with the fundamental, and the relative strengths of the fundamental and the different overtones determine an instrument's tonal characteristics—why, for example, the tone of a flute is so different from that of a violin.

Example 36

Overtone Series starting on C

Chords in 4ths

It is possible, however, to ignore the overtone series and build chords from other intervals; and the most common of such chords are chords in fourths, cuartal harmonies.

Chords in fourths are normally written in three-, four-, or five-note versions. Such chords sound fairly consonant because they contain only the notes of the pentatonic scale, and there are no minor second intervals—the most dissonant interval—in the pentatonic scale.

Example 37

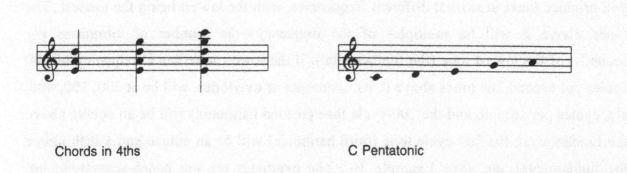

Chords in 4ths   C Pentatonic

Versions with six or more notes are generally not used, as they sound somewhat dissonant due to the presence of the transposed minor second interval.

Example 38

Cuartal harmonies can be inverted, but when inversions are used, the preponderant interval should still be the fourth in order that the chord retain its character. If too many other intervals are present, the chord will sound like an added-note chord or an inversion of a tertian harmony (especially if you're using both chords in thirds and chords in fourths in a progression; using only chords in fourths will minimize this problem).

Because chords in fourths are symmetric, they sound unsettled, ambiguous. For that reason, they tend to blend well with chords in thirds. Cuartal harmonies progress easily to tertian harmonies and vice versa. In progressions utilizing both tertian and cuartal harmonies, one or more notes in a preceding chord are often present in the following chord when the progression moves from a tertian to a cuartal harmony, or vice versa.

Example 39

It's also possible to combine augmented fourths with perfect fourths when using cuartal harmonies. When an augmented fourth (tritone) is present, it's usually at the top of the chord, and the two notes comprising it often act as leading tones; such chords normally resolve (if they resolve—they can just as easily progress to another similar chord) by movement of a minor second in one of the upper two voices.

Example 40

Cuartal harmonies also lend themselves to parallelism. (See page 43.)

Example 41

Two works which make use of chords in fourths are Arnold Schoenberg's *Chamber Symphony*, Opus 9, and Herbie Hancock's "Maiden Voyage." Keith Jarrett and McCoy Tyner also make extensive use of cuartal harmonies in their music, with the *Sama Lucaya* album being a good example of Tyner's work.

Clusters

You can also write chords based on the interval of the second. Such chords are called *clusters* and are useful, among other things, for producing percussive effects. Clusters are often written using the notes of a scale, and such clusters sound relatively open; denser-sounding clusters can be produced by filling in the spaces between scale notes. Clusters, however, are not always produced by using the notes of a scale; they can be formed just as easily from arbitrarily chosen notes.

Example 42

In the first bar, two ways of writing a cluster containing the notes D, E, F, G, A, and B; in the second bar, two ways of writing a cluster containing D, D♯, E, F, F♯, G, G♯, A, A♯, B, and B♯ (C).

You can use clusters in progressions involving chords built from thirds and fourths, but when you do, take care to make sure that your clusters appear in relatively dissonant settings; otherwise, they'll sound out of place, jarring. When you want a shock effect, though, a loud cluster in a consonant setting is about as effective a device as you'll find.

You can use clusters in the same manner as 9-, 10-, and 11-note rows to set up entrances using notes not found in the clusters (and/or rows). When notes are not sounded in repeated clusters, they can be used to good effect as the beginnings of new passages.

A useful thing to remember when using clusters is that the ear will not hear the internal notes of a cluster as individual tones. This is especially true if the cluster is played by a group of similar instruments such as strings, or by an instrument like the piano. The ear will, however, notice gaps within a cluster, and the larger the gaps, the more noticeable they'll be.

A good example of a work making extensive use of clusters is Bartok's *Fourth String Quartet*. The entire work is filled with clusters; see, for example, page 11. Charlie Mingus' "Sue's Changes," from his *Changes One* album, is a good example of a popular piece which makes fairly extensive use of (piano) clusters.

Chord Symbols

Chord symbols are a type of musical shorthand. A player should (ideally) be able to read any chord symbol and know instantly which notes are in the chord it symbolizes. The following table, using middle C as the starting point, lists all of the chords and chord symbols you'll normally encounter. (There are no symbols for chords in fourths or for clusters; and the following symbols are only used in jazz, rock, and other types of popular music—you won't find them in classical music or in "serious" [academic] contemporary music.)

Example 43

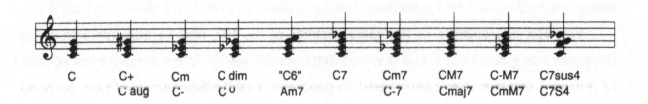

C	C+	Cm	C dim	"C6"	C7	Cm7	CM7	C-M7	C7sus4
	C aug	C-	C º	Am7		C-7	Cmaj7	CmM7	C7S4

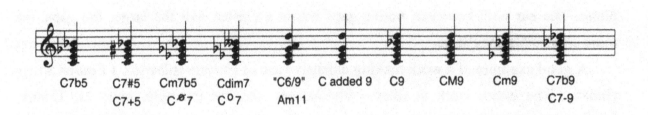

C7b5	C7#5	Cm7b5	Cdim7	"C6/9"	C added 9	C9	CM9	Cm9	C7b9
C7+5	C ø7	C º7		Am11					C7-9

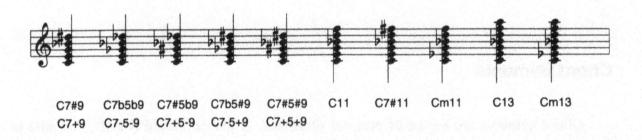

C7#9	C7b5b9	C7#5b9	C7b5#9	C7#5#9	C11	C7#11	Cm11	C13	Cm13
C7+9	C7-5-9	C7+5-9	C7-5+9	C7+5+9					

To find the notes in chords with roots other than C, measure the intervals between C and the notes above it in any given type of chord and use those intervals with the new root. For instance, looking at the chord Cm you'll see that the notes in it are C, E♭, and G; the interval between C and E♭ is a minor third, and the interval between E♭ and G is a major third. If you'd want to find the notes in the chord Fm you would use F as the root and go up a minor third (to A♭) and from there up a major third (to C). The *intervals* between the notes in a C minor chord are exactly the same as the *intervals* between the notes in an F minor chord.

You'll also sometimes run across chord symbols which use Roman numerals. These are academic symbols and are fairly simple once you understand them. The Roman numerals correspond to the notes in the scale upon which chords are rooted. When no additional notation is added, an upper case Roman numeral means that a chord is major; a lower case numeral means that the chord is minor. When a plus sign appears to the right of an upper case numeral, it means that the chord is augmented. When a small circle appears to the right of a lower case numeral, it means that the chord is diminished.

Example 44

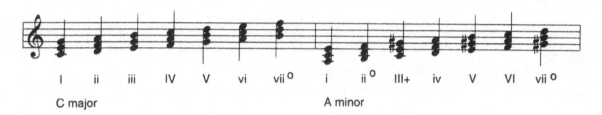

Note: The III chord in minor is often played as a major, rather than as an augmented, chord.

Arabic numbers to the right of a lower case Roman numeral indicate how far above the note in the bass—which is *not* necessarily the root of the chord (see "Inversions," page 23)—the other notes in the chord are. For example, a dominant (V) "six-four-three" chord in the key of C (see below) would contain D in the bass, F (a third above D), G (the root—a fourth above D), and B (a sixth above D).

Example 45

If all of this sounds complicated, don't worry about it. Chances are good that unless your masochistic tendencies get the better of you and you decide to plow through some academic theory texts, you'll rarely if ever need to use this information.

Solos

Only certain types of scales will "work" with certain types of chords, and the types that are appropriate depend on context. Even given these limitations, a wide selection of scales is available to the improviser. The following table lists all common chords and some scales which work with them. This, though, is not a comprehensive list; it's always possible to invent new synthetic scales which will work with various types of chords. For example, you could add the note E♭ to the C whole tone scale and come up with a new scale which would work quite well with a C7♭5 chord.

Suggestion: When experimenting with scales, use them singly; don't combine them until you're used to their individual sounds/characteristics.

Table 5
(Chord types are in bold type; scales are in normal type)

Major	Minor	Diminished	Augmented
Major	Natural Minor	Locrian	Augmented
Lydian	Harmonic Minor	Diminished	Enigmatic
Mixolydian	Melodic Minor	Overtone Blues	Spanish Phrygian
Diminished	Dorian	Hungarian Minor	Spanish Locrian
Augmented	Phrygian	Super Locrian	Whole Tone Blues
Overtone	Diminished	Spanish Locrian	Whole Tone
Spanish Phrygian	Augmented	Whole Tone Blues	
Pentatonic	Spanish Phrygian		
Blues	Pentatonic		
Overtone Blues	Blues		
Whole Tone Blues	Overtone Blues		
	Hungarian Minor		
	Whole Tone Blues		

Minor 7th	Minor 7♭5	Dominant 7th (V7)	Major 7th
Natural Minor	Diminished	Mixolydian	Major
Melodic Minor	Locrian	Diminished	Lydian
Overtone Blues	Super Locrian	Blues	Augmented
Dorian	Spanish Locrian	Overtone Blues	Pentatonic
Phrygian	Blues	Whole Tone Blues	
Spanish Phrygian	Overtone Blues	Spanish Phrygian	
Pentatonic			
Blues			
Whole Tone Blues			

7♭5
Overtone
Blues
Overtone Blues
Whole Tone
Diminished
Enigmatic
Oriental
Spanish Locrian

7#5
Whole Tone
Whole Tone Blues
Enigmatic
Spanish Locrian

Diminished 7th
Diminished
Overtone Blues

Half Diminshed 7th
Locrian
Spanish Locrian
Whole Tone Blues
Super Locrian
Overtone Blues
Diminished

Minor-Major 7th
Harmonic Minor
Melodic Minor
Hungarian Minor
Augmented

9th
Mixolydian
Pentatonic
Overtone
Spanish Phrygian
Blues
Overtone Blues
Whole Tone Blues

Major 9th
Major
Lydian
Pentatonic
Augmented

Minor 9th
Natural Minor
Melodic Minor
Dorian
Pentatonic
Blues
Overtone Blues
Wholetone Blues

7♭9
Diminished
Spanish Phrygian
Blues
Oriental

7#9
Diminished
Pentatonic
Spanish Phrygian
Blues
Overtone Blues
Whole Tone Blues

11th
Mixolydian
Overtone Blues
Whole Tone Blues
Blues
Pentatonic
Spanish Phrygian

Minor 11th
Natural Minor
Dorian
Pentatonic
Blues
Overtone Blues
Whole Tone Blues

7#11
Pentatonic
Diminished
Overtone
Whole Tone
Blues
Overtone Blues
Whole Tone Blues

13th
Mixolydian
Pentatonic
Diminished
Overtone
Blues
Overtone Blues

Chords in 4ths
Dorian
Phrygian
Myxolidian
Natural Minor
Pentatonic
Locrian
Spanish Phrygian
Blues
Overtone Blues
Oriental

Clusters
Almost any scale,
depending on what
kind of effect you
want

Note: Where the pentatonic scale is indicated for the various types of minor chords, this does *not* mean the diatonic pentatonic. Rather, it means (a) form(s) of the pentatonic with a minor 3rd.

3

Chord Progressions

Theoretically, any chord can progress to any other chord. But in practice, certain chords typically progress to certain others, and some chords are more important than others. The most important chords are I, IV, and V—thousands of songs have been written using nothing but these three chords. (Chord progressions in almost all pieces, from rock to classical, can be summarized as I–IV–V–I, or, even more simply, as I–V–I.)

The progression of chords derived from major and (harmonic) minor scales is very similar. The following table covers chords derived from both scales, and for the sake of convenience uses only upper case Roman numerals. Note that the VII chord (vii diminished, actually) functions as an incomplete V7 chord; so, it's not treated here as a fully independent chord. Note also that the most frequent progressions involve movement of a second, fourth, or fifth—these are the strongest root (chord) progressions; root progressions of a third or sixth are much weaker.

Table 6

Chord	Progresses to (in approximate order of frequency)
I	V, IV, VI, II, III
II	V, VI, I, III, IV
III	VI, IV, II, I, V
IV	V, I, VI, II, III
V	I, VI, IV, II, III
VI	V, II, III, IV, I
VII	I, VI, III, II, IV

Certain other chords frequently appear in progressions using chords derived from major and minor scales. The most common are the Neapolitan sixth and the augmented sixth chords. (The somewhat odd term, Neapolitan sixth, has its roots in the fact that opera composers in Naples used the chord [in first inversion and symbolized as ♭II6 or N6] extensively around the turn of the 18th century.) The Neapolitan sixth is a ♭II major chord and is basically a substitute for the IV chord in that it almost always progresses to the V chord, although occasionally—especially in jazz harmonies—it will progress to the I chord

Example 46

N6 in C major   N6 in G minor

Augmented sixth chords are always rooted on the flatted sixth degree of the scale and get their name from the intervals they contain. The distance from their roots to their highest notes is an augmented sixth, which sounds the same as a minor seventh, but is spelled differently. Like Neapolitan sixths, augmented sixths function as substitutes for the IV chord; also, as with Neapolitan sixths, the progression of augmented sixths is rather restricted. They often appear in cadence formulas and usually progress to the V chord, though sometimes they progress to the I chord's second inversion, which is normally followed by the V and then by the I in root position.

Augmented sixths come in three types, called (for no good reason whatsoever) the German 6th, Italian 6th, and French 6th. The difference between the three is that the German sixth contains exactly the same notes as a dominant 7th (though it's spelled differently, and is rooted a half step up from the actual dominant seventh); the Italian 6th is different from the German 6th only in that it does not contain a fifth (just a root, third, and augmented 6th); and the French 6th differs from the German 6th in that it contains a raised fourth rather than a perfect fifth, and sounds like the familiar 7♭5 chord in jazz harmonies (though it's spelled differently and functions differently).

Example 47

It6   G6   F6

Augmented sixth chords in the key of C

In practice, all you need to remember is that augmented sixth chords are rooted on the lowered sixth degree of a scale, sound like dominant seventh (V7) chords, but function as substitutes for the IV chord, and normally progress to the V chord, or, less frequently, to the I chord.

Voice Leading

If you're writing arrangements, you'll want to keep what's called *voice leading* in mind. This means thinking of the interior notes in chord progressions as melodies rather than simply as filler between the bass and soprano (melody) lines. Your progressions will sound smoother if you keep the following principles in mind when writing arrangements:

1) Movement of parts (voices) should be primarily by whole step or half step intervals.

2) After leaps, there should be immediate movement in the opposite direction.

3) Avoid crossing parts.

Example 48

Part Crossing

4) Avoid parallel and hidden octaves and perfect fifths, especially between outer parts. (Hidden octaves and fifths are produced when two parts moving in parallel motion move into an octave or fifth.)

Example 49

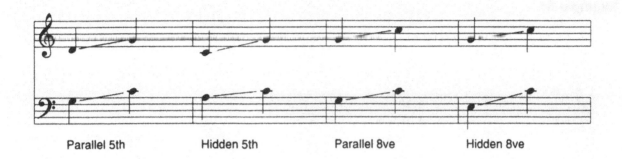

Parallel 5th   Hidden 5th   Parallel 8ve   Hidden 8ve

5) Oblique and contrary motion are generally to be preferred to similar and parallel motion.

Example 50

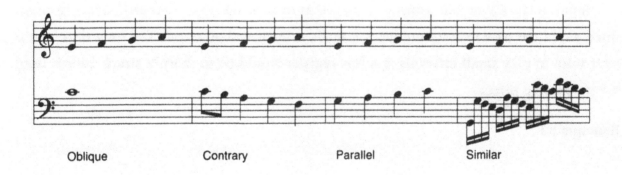

Oblique   Contrary   Parallel   Similar

6) Avoid upward leaps at the tops of ascending lines, and downward leaps at the bottoms of descending lines.

7) Avoid consecutive leaps, especially in the same direction.

<u>Note</u>: If you follow these rules, you should write good sounding progressions. But these rules are not iron-clad—if you have a good musical reason for doing so, break them.

Spacing

As a general rule, the distance between adjacent notes in a chord should never exceed an octave, the one exception being the distance from the bass to the next higher note.

Example 51

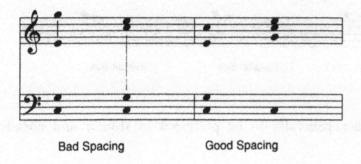

Bad Spacing   Good Spacing

Small intervals should always be placed at or near the tops of chords. Placing small intervals in the bass register produces a muddy, unattractive sound. The only time you'd ever want to play small intervals in a low register would be in sharply struck chords used for percussive effect.

Example 52

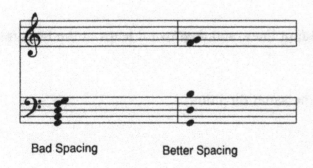

Bad Spacing   Better Spacing

Substitutions

The I, IV and V are the most important chords. The other chords derived from the major and minor scales largely function as substitutes for these three chords.

Table 7

Chord	Substitutes
I	VI, rarely III
IV	II, less often VI (and occasionally N6, G6, It6, or F6)
V	VII, rarely III (and in jazz harmonies occasionally ♭II or ♭II7)

As progressions of chords derived from the major and minor scales are very similar, it follows that chords from the major scale can be substituted for chords from the minor scale (in progressions utilizing chords built from the minor scale) and vice versa. For example, chords derived from the C minor scale can be substituted for chords derived from the C major scale. Composers have made use of this principle since the mid 19th century. The most common substitution of this type is the substitution of the minor iv chord for the major IV chord. You have to be careful, though, when making such substitutions, as it's easy to end up with jarring, "wrong" sounding progressions if you make major/minor substitutions without a good musical reason for doing so.

In jazz, it's fairly common to find chords written/played without a root (especially for guitar and piano). What this does in effect is to substitute a chord a third above the (unplayed) root of the original chord for the original chord—though it could be argued that these are often not real substitutions, as the root of the original chord is normally supplied by a bass guitar or string bass.

Example 53

C7 substitute E dim   C7 substitute Em7b5

Another common jazz substitution is that of chords containing flatted fifths—chords of this type can be substituted for similar chords whose root is a flatted fifth away. The most common such substitution is that of 7♭5 chords a tritone apart. Again, it could be argued that the substitution of 7♭5 chords a tritone apart is not a real substitution, because such chords contain the same notes, though the chords are spelled differently. For example, the notes in C7♭5 chord are exactly the same as the notes in a G♭7♭5 chord.

Example 54

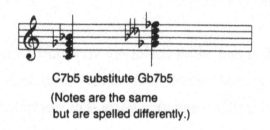

C7b5 substitute Gb7b5

(Notes are the same
but are spelled differently.)

7♭5 Substitution

Still another common substitution is that of using the ♭II7 chord in place of the V7 chord. Any dominant 7th-type (V7-type) chord can be replaced by the dominant 7th-type chord a flatted fifth away. For example, in the key of C the G7 (V7) chord can be replaced by a D♭7 (♭II7) chord. (Notice that the third and seventh degrees—F and B [C♭]—are identical in those two chords.

Example 55

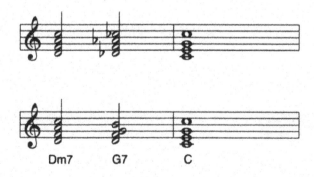

Dm7   G7   C

Dominant 7th-type Substitution

The methods of finding substitutes we've already considered involve individual chords. Another method involves strings of chords; here you take a melody and work backward from a cadence. You find chords containing the melody notes and reconstruct the progression using the strongest possible substitutes. (Remember that progression by seconds, fourths, and fifths is strongest.) Of course, this method of substitution is more useful when writing arrangements than when improvising. The following example shows the final three measures of a simple melody and two very different progressions which both "fit."

Example 56

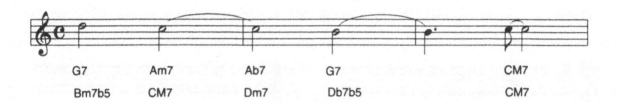

G7	Am7	Ab7	G7		CM7
Bm7b5	CM7	Dm7	Db7b5		CM7

Modulation

Modulating (moving) from one key to another is easy. It's done through the use of *pivot chords*. Pivot chords are chords which are found in two keys—the key being modulated from, and the key being modulated to. As a rule, there should be one or two pivot chords before a modulation takes place, that is, before a V–I progression occurs in the new key. In other words, you can change keys most easily by having one or two chords which can be interpreted as being in either the new key or the old key followed by a V–I progress in the new key. The I in the new key should be on a strong beat, normally the first beat of a measure.

Example 57

Key of C: I   vi   I$^6_4$
Key of G: IV   ii   IV$^6_4$ V$^6_5{}_3$ I

The easiest keys to modulate to and from are the *near-related* keys, that is keys with scales containing all but one of the same notes as the key being modulated *from*. The reason for this is that such keys have several chords in common, chords which can act as pivot chords. The following example shows G major and its near-related keys.

Example 58

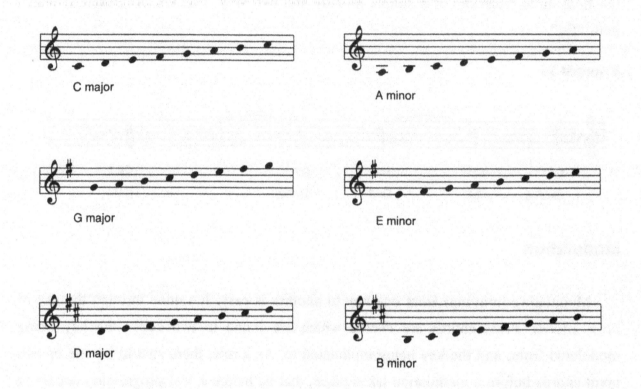

C major

A minor

G major

E minor

D major

B minor

It is possible to modulate without the use of pivot chords. Such modulations are called *abrupt modulations* and are generally produced through the introduction of the V chord of the new key without advance preparation, that is, without pivot chords. Abrupt modulations tend to sound jarring and should be used with care.

Another type of abrupt modulation is also common. In this type, even the introduction of the new V chord is omitted. At the beginning of a new section (at the second repetition of a 32-measure AABA song pattern, for instance) the entire pattern is shifted upward—generally a major or minor second—and the remainder of the piece is then finished in the new, higher key. It's an effective device if it's not overused—but it's easy to overuse and has, in fact, become a cheesy pop music cliche.

Cadences

Cadences are chord patterns that mark the end of phrases, sections, and pieces. There are four common types:

1) Authentic cadences end in the progression V–I; and the V is often preceded by the II or IV. The authentic cadence is the most final sounding and the most common type of cadence.

Example 59

Authentic Cadence

2) Half cadences end on the V chord. Because of that they sound inconclusive and imply further movement. The V chord is normally preceded by the II or IV.

Example 60

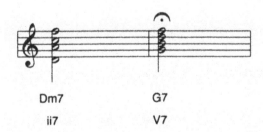

Half Cadence

3) Plagal cadences end in the progression IV–I and are normally softer and less final sounding than authentic cadences. The "amen" at the end of many hymn tunes is a familiar example of the plagal cadence.

Example 61

C   F   C

I   IV$\frac{6}{4}$ I

Plagal Cadence

4) Deceptive cadences end in the progression V–vi, with the V often preceded by the ii or IV. They're somewhat surprising and not as final sounding as authentic cadences. Deceptive cadences can serve as either a means of harmonic diversity or as a means of introducing a new key—with the vi chord as the i chord of the new key—if the new key is affirmed (with an authentic cadence). An interesting example of the deceptive cadence is the song "Mongoloid," by Devo, the body of which is really nothing but a repeated deceptive cadence (vi–I–IV–V–VI/vi).

Example 62

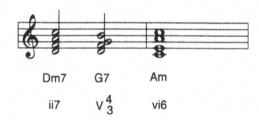

Dm7   G7   Am

ii7   V$\frac{4}{3}$ vi6

Deceptive Cadence

Cycle of Fifths

Key signatures can be arranged in a circle with all of the keys (major scales) a perfect fifth apart; that is, the first note in any given major scale will be the fifth note of the preceding scale. This is called *the cycle of fifths*. Progressions in jazz standards are often based on the cycle of fifths—Am7, D9, Gm7, C9, etc., for example. A few standards utilizing the cycle of fifths are "Satin Doll," "The Shadow of Your Smile," and "Laura."

Example 63

Parallelism

"Parallelism," one of the better descriptive terms in music, refers to a type of chord movement found in both jazz and 20th-century "serious" music. It refers to the parallel movement of chords—usually of identical-type chords (that is, all the intervals in them are identical).

"Real" parallelism is the most common type of parallelism. It refers to the parallel movement of identical-type chords. The chords can be of any type, and the motion of the chords can be uniformly upward or downward, or it can alternate between upward and downward movement as long as all voices (notes in the chords) move by identical intervals.

Example 64

Real Parallelism

The other common type of parallelism is "tonal" parallelism, in which (as in normal tonal practice) chords are built from the notes of a scale, and thus sometimes move in *similar* rather than strictly *parallel* motion. As well, the chord types in this variety of "parallelism" are not identical.

Example 65

Tonal Parallelism

A hybrid type—a variety of "real" parallelism—utilizes movement of identical-type chords to preserve a feeling of tonality or modality by outlining a scale with their movement. The following progression outlines E Dorian in the top voice (plus B Dorian and F♯ Dorian in the middle and bottom voices). While chords in fourths are used here, any type of chord can be used; and the time values of the chords can be similar or dissimilar.

Example 66

Harmonizing Rows

There are several ways of harmonizing 12-tone rows. The row in the following example, for instance, can be harmonized in a number of ways.

Example 67

1) The standard way to harmonize rows it to take any give note and to combine it with as many of the preceding or following notes in the row as you wish, remembering not to skip or repeat any notes:

Example 68

2) An alternative type of harmonization—a form of parallelism—is to pick a type of chord and to have the notes in the row always take a certain position (root, for example) in the chords. For instance, you could have all of the notes in a row be the top notes in three-note chords in fourths. (Any type of chord—7th, 9th, cluster, etc.—can be used.)

Example 69

3) A variation of this type of harmonization is to allow the notes in a row to be in any position (root, third, fifth, etc.) in a given type of chord.

Example 70

4) Another variation is to have the notes in the row always be the roots (or top notes) of chords, but to vary the types of chords.

Example 71

5) Still another way is to harmonize randomly, letting the notes in the row be in any position in chords of your choosing.

Example 72

Note: Moving notes in a row up or down an octave or two—or three—is perfectly acceptable.

4

Melody

The following guidelines are applicable to both written melodies and improvised solos:

1) Rhythmic activity should either remain at the same level or increase during the course of a melody/solo. This is especially true of improvised solos: if you begin a solo at a blazingly fast pace, you'll have nowhere to go.

2) Sequences—patterns of notes repeated at different pitch levels—are a useful and easy way to produce coherence in a melody. Sequences, however, should not be overused; sequence patterns should be repeated no more than three or four times in a row, as more repetitions tend to sound boring. The final repetition of a sequence (usually the third) should be varied.

Example 73

3) Sequences are also handy devices for modulating. The sequence in the previous example, for instance, can be made to modulate to E with only very minor changes to the end of the third repetition.

Example 74

4) Exact repetition of a pattern at the same pitch level more than three or four times in a row should be avoided. Excessive repetition of patterns, while an easy way to construct solos, indicates a lack of imagination. Avoid playing patterns such as the following:

Example 75

The one exception to the above rule is that such patterns can be used to set up solos. Repetitious patterns sound (and are) boring, so if you use one at the beginning of a solo, the remainder of it will tend to sound fresh—it will be a welcome relief from the monotony of the repeating pattern.

5) Imitation—not exact repetition—of previously used patterns is an effective means of producing coherence in a melody.

Example 76

6) Excessive repetition of the same note should be avoided, except where, as with repetitious patterns, it is used to set up solos.

7) The range (from highest to lowest note) should be at least a perfect fifth.

8) Two or more large leaps (a fourth or larger) in succession in the same direction should be avoided.

9) After a leap, the melody should immediately move by step (major or minor second) in the opposite direction.

Example 77

Incorrect   Correct

10) The highest note in a melody should be held and/or accented.

11) The highest note should be sounded only once.

12) If there are two high points, the higher one should come second.

13) Break any of these rules if there's a good musical reason for doing so.

Melody Types

Melodies usually come in one of six shapes:

1) They begin low and proceed higher.

Example 78

2) They begin high and proceed lower.

Example 79

3) They begin low, reach a high point 60%–80% of the way through, and then go back down. (This is the most common type.)

Example 80

4) They begin low, reach a high point, descend, then reach a second high point higher than the first, and then descend.

Example 81

5) They begin high, reach a low point 60%–80% of the way through, and then reascend.

Example 82

6) They center around a certain note. It's generally best to avoid this type because, unless great care is taken, this type of melody sounds repetitious.

Example 83

<u>Note</u>: For space conservation reasons, all of the melodies in the above examples are very short. Melodies in actual pieces tend to be longer than those in the examples.

Melodic Variations

There are several ways to get additional mileage out of a melody:

Example 84

Original Melody

1) Augmentation—multiplying the note (time) values of a melody.

Example 85

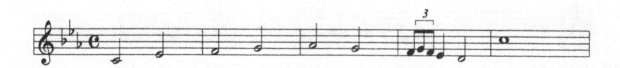

Augmentation Doubling Note Values

2) Diminution—dividing the note values of a melody.

Example 86

Diminution Halving Note Values

3) Inversion—playing a melody upside down.

Example 87

Inversion

4) Retrograde—playing a melody backward. (A retrograde melody, however, is not generally recognizable as being related to the original melody.)

Example 88

Retrograde

5) Retrograde Inversion—playing a melody backward and upside down. (A melody manipulated in this manner will almost certainly be unrecognizable as being related to the original melody. Primarily for this reason, retrograde inversions are normally used only with 12-tone rows.)

Example 89

Retrograde Inversion

5

Form

Blues

The most important form in American popular music is blues form, which is basically quite simple—it's a 12-bar, repeating chord pattern in 4/4 time—but the number of variations on it are virtually endless. The basic blues pattern utilizes dominant 7th-type (V7-type) chords on the first, fourth and fifth degrees of the scale (in other words, as the I, IV, and V chords) in the following manner, with each chord having a duration of one measure:

Example 90

I7   I7   I7   I7   IV7   IV7   I7   I7   V7   IV7   I7   I7

There are a large number of common variations on this pattern. One is to use 9th and/or 13th chords in place of the 7th chords. Another is to replace the second measure of I7 with IV7:

Example 91

I7   IV7   I7   I7   IV7   IV7   I7   I7   V7   IV7   I7   I7

A third, when using 9th chords in places of 7ths, is to replace the IV9 (IV7) in the 10th bar with a ♭VI9 on the first two beats and a V9 on the second two, and then to replace the I7 on the final two beats in the 12th bar with a V7♯9:

Example 92

I7 IV9 I7 I7 IV9 IV9 I7 I7 V9 ♭VI9/V9 I7 I7/V7♯9

A less common variation is to replace bars 7 through 10 with (bar 7) I7-IIm7, (bar 8) IIIm7-♭IIIm7, (bar 9) V9, (bar 10) ♭VI9-V9, and then to replace the final two bars of I7 with a "turnaround" (see page 56 for a discussion of turnarounds):

Example 93

I7 IV9 I7 I7 IV9 IV9 I7/ii7 iii7/♭iii7 V9 ♭VI9/V9 (turnaround)

A nice example of this variation can be found on "Stormy Monday" on *The Allman Brothers Band at Fillmore East* album (though they use a ♭VI major 7th in place of ♭VI9/V9 in bar 10, which is very unusual, as major 7ths are almost never used in blues progressions).

One very common variation on the blues pattern is the "minor" blues, in which the dominant 7th-type chords are replaced by minor 7th chords.

Example 94

i7 i7 i7 i7 iv7 iv7 i7 i7 v7 iv7 i7 i7

Still another way to vary the blues pattern is to change the number of bars in it to any number chosen by the composer. Most frequently this is done in "jazz blues." One example of this blues pattern variation is the song "Le Lis" on Billy Cobham's *Spectrum* album, which is basically a 24-bar minor blues with a couple of nice chord changes beyond those in a normal minor blues.

Yet another way to vary the blues pattern is to use a time signature other than 4/4. This is most commonly done in jazz blues, where you'll find blues tunes with time signatures like 5/4 and 7/4.

Perhaps the most common blues variation is "rock blues," which is ordinarily played faster than normal blues (if there is such a thing), and which is played in true 4/4 time. That is, in rock blues, eighth notes are played evenly rather than "swung," as in normal blues. (Even though blues tunes, when written out, are normally notated as being in 4/4, they're usually played as if they're in 12/8; that is, the eighth notes in most blues tunes are "swung"—they're played like triplets. For example, on a beat with two eighth notes, the first eighth note would be held twice as long as the second. This gives the blues its characteristic "shuffle" sound.) There are thousands of rock blues songs, but a particularly good example of the genre is "Sound the Bell," from Johnny Winter's *Serious Business* album.

Many rock and roll songs are also based on the blues, the songs of Little Richard and Chuck Berry being good examples. Like rock blues, blues-oriented rock tunes are normally played fast and with "straight" eighth notes, but their chord structure often varies from that of the normal blues pattern. A famous example of blues-oriented rock is Chuck Berry's "Johnny B. Goode," which is basically two 12-bar blues patterns set back to back, with the IV7 chord in the 10th measure replaced by a V7 chord.

The *turnaround* is an important adjunct to blues form. Turnarounds are cadence formulas and replace the final two bars of I7 in blues form. Most turnarounds are based on the progression I–vi–ii–V, with each chord taking up half a measure. There are many variations on this basic pattern. Here are a few:

Example 95

I7—VI7♯5♯9—ii7—V13

I7—IV9—I7—V7♯9

iii7—vi7—ii7—V7

IM7—VI9—ii7—V9

III7♯9—VI13—II7♯9—V13

IM7—♭IIIM7—IIM7—♭IIM7

<u>Note</u>: It's fairly common for blues tunes to begin with the last four bars of the blues progression, including a turnaround. Turnarounds are also commonly used with songs in other forms.

Bar Form

Bar form, or AABA form, is another frequently encountered song form. This form is normally 32 measures long, with all four sections being of equal length—eight measures. (Eight-measure sections are the norm for non-blues song forms in American popular music.) Examples of AABA form are very numerous; "Well You Needn't," by Thelonius Monk, is a good example.

ABAC

ABAC form is also fairly common, although not so common as either blues form or bar form. Like bar (AABA) form, ABAC form is usually 32 measures long and is divided into four eight-bar sections. "Green Dolphin Street" is an example of this form.

Binary

Songs in binary form—AA' or AB—are also common. (The difference between A' and B is that A' is similar to A, while B is contrasting.) Both sections are normally eight measures long. An example of AA' form is "There Will Never Be Another You" (A and A' are both 16 bars long, though, in this song), while an example of AB form is "Jelly Roll," by Thelonius Monk.

Ternary

Occasionally songs are written in ternary form—ABA or ABA'. Again, all sections are usually eight measures long. "Lullaby of Birdland" (ABA), by George Shearing, and "Bluesette" (ABA'), by Toots Thielman, are examples of this relatively rare (in popular music) form.

Classical Forms

There are a number of forms used in classical music which could be of use to jazz and rock musicians, the two most potentially useful probably being the *rondo* and *arch* forms.

Rondo form is very common in classical music, and in its simplest form is ABACA form. There are, however, very few examples of rondo form in popular music; the best known example is "Blue Rondo a la Turk," on Dave Brubeck's *Time Out* album.

Arch form, ABCBA form, is the central organizing feature in Bartok's deservedly famous *Fourth String Quartet*. It's used there, however, on a macro scale, with materials from the first movement reappearing in the fifth movement, and materials from the second movement reappearing in the fourth, giving the piece an overall ABCBA form—there's no reason, though, that arch form could not also be used as a song form. But as useful as it potentially is, I can't think of a single example of arch form in popular music. So, it seems like a fruitful area for exploration.

<u>Note</u>: A useful exercise for aspiring songwriters is to go through a fake book and to figure out the forms of the songs in it; and a good place to start is with careful examination of the examples listed above. Also, there is no reason other than convention that sections or phrases should be eight measures long. If you're writing songs, you'd do well to experiment with phrases of different lengths.

6

Useful Techniques

This chapter could just as easily be titled "Tricks of the Trade." It's a catalog of devices which are useful in composition and improvisation. All are easy to apply, but not all are in common use—at least in popular music. So, using some of the more uncommon "tricks of the trade" is a good way to give your music a distinctive sound.

Ostinato

An ostinato is a repeating pattern. Ostinatos can be used in rhythms, bass lines, chord progressions, and melodic figures. They're musical glue—they hold things together. With an ostinato going on, you can get away with playing almost *anything* over it. Unfortunately, that's well known, and an amazing number of terrible pieces utilizing ostinatos have been written. (Tune your radio to any pop station for an excruciating example.) The best known ostinato-based piece is probably *Bolero* by Ravel—but even it has the redeeming feature of good orchestration; many other ostinato-based pieces are infinitely worse. Two well known, and somewhat better than average, ostinato-based pop songs are "Chameleon," by Herbie Hancock, and "Superstition," by Stevie Wonder. (Hancock uses a bass ostinato in the long intro section and short concluding section of "Chameleon"; and Wonder uses a melodic ostinato throughout "Superstition," but only when in the tonic.) Don't let the preceding comments deter you, though; ostinatos can be very useful—but only if they're not overused.

Example 96

Rhythmic Ostinato

Bass Ostinato

Harmonic Ostinato

Melodic Ostinato

Pedal Tone

The rather obscure term "pedal tone" comes from the practice of holding long bass notes with the foot pedals on pipe organs. It refers to a note which is held throughout an entire piece, or section(s) of a piece. Like ostinatos, pedal tones serve to hold things together, but because of their static nature they're less effective at doing so than ostinatos. Pedal tones can be on any pitch, but are most commonly in the bass register. The drone in some types of folk music is a familiar example of pedal tone use. The following example shows a pedal tone in the bass.

Example 97

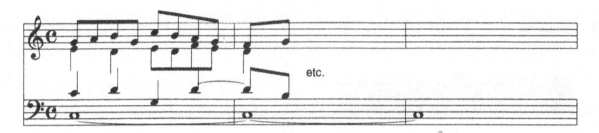

Pedal Tone

Hocket

Hocket (from the Latin word for "hiccup") is a device in which notes are rapidly alternated between two or more voices or instruments (voices usually). It can produce a very pleasant and unusual effect, especially when the voices and/or instruments are well separated on the stage. Example 98 shows a short melodic fragment and how it might look if broken up by hocket. (Strict one-for-one tradeoffs are common, but the alternations can be arranged in other ways, e.g., two-notes-for-two-notes, two-for-one, three-for-two, etc., etc.)

Example 98

Hocket

Pointillism

Pointillism is a technique which consists of breaking up a melody by displacing many or all of the notes in it by an octave or two (or three) up or down, and, perhaps, altering the dynamics and articulation of the notes as well. The following example subjects the melodic fragment in the previous (hocket) example to pointillistic treatment.

Example 99

Pointillism

Tone Color Melody

Tone color melody is produced by taking a melodic line and breaking it up into very short segments, often as short as one or two notes, played by different instruments. It's often combined with pointillism and can be a very striking effect. Webern's arrangement of the ricercar from Bach's *Musical Offering* is a good example of tone color melody.

Example 100

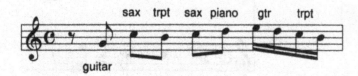

Tone Color Melody

Mirrors

To produce mirrors, begin with any given pitch level and then match every note played above it with one below it (at the same intervalic distance below the original pitch as the intervalic distance above it of the note it's mirroring), and vice versa—or, as Vincent Persichetti puts it in *Twentieth Century Harmony*, mirrors consist of producing "strictly inverted intervals in symmetrical reflection." (If all of this sounds confusing, a glance at Example 101 should instantly clarify the matter.)

In mirrors, one side can lead the other or they can proceed simultaneously. Mirrors can be used both melodically and harmonically (with chords). In mirrors for keyboard instruments, it's best to start on either D or G♯ because the fingering will be the same for both hands if the starting pitch is one of those notes. For a good example of mirror writing, see the flute parts on page one of Bartok's *Concerto for Orchestra*.

Example 101

Mirror Writing

Doubling

One of the easiest and most pleasing effects available is the doubling of melodic lines in thirds, sixths, or octaves. In such runs, notes from the same scale are almost always used in both lines. Although runs in thirds, sixths, and octaves are the most common, runs doubled at other intervals are usable, and it's a good idea to experiment with them. Good examples of doubled runs (between two guitars) can be found on many cuts by the Allman

Brothers, "Hot Lanta," on *Allman Brothers Live at Fillmore East,* being one such track. For examples of octave doubling on a single instrument (guitar), listen to virtually any cut on Wes Montgomery's later albums.

Example 102

Doubling

A variation is to have the doubling voice or instrument maintain a constant interval between itself and the melodic voice or instrument. This gives the effect of playing in two keys simultaneously. The following example has an E major melody in the top voice, with the doubling voice a constant major third below it in C major.

Example 103

Doubling At Constant Interval

Tradeoffs

Antiphony (the use of tradeoffs) is an ancient device. It consists of question-and-answer phrases played (or sung) by different instruments (or voices). In improvisation, these phrases are generally either two or four measures in length and are called *tradeoffs.* They tend to work best when the trading off instruments (or voices) are well separated. One example of tradeoffs can be found at the end of "Work Song" on Paul Butterfield's *East West* album.

Example 104

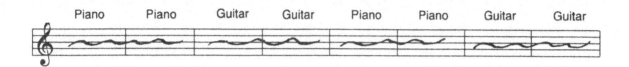

Tradeoffs (solos)

Canon

Canon is a contrapuntal device in which a melody in one voice or instrument is exactly imitated by another voice or instrument after a certain amount of time has passed—one measure is most usual. The imitating voice can be at any pitch level, but it's most common (and easiest) for it to be at the unison—same exact notes as the original melody—or an octave above or below the first voice.

Canons are not common in popular music, but one example, "Canon," can be found on Charlie Mingus' *Mingus Moves* album. The following example consists of the first few bars of a canon at the octave utilizing the C blues scale.

Example 105

Canon

Rhythmic Variation

Probably 90% of popular music is in 4/4 time, with most of the rest in 3/4; but there's no law dictating that songs be written in those time signatures. Music in 5/8 or 7/4, for example, sounds refreshingly different, although it's hard to dance to—at least for those accustomed to hearing only music in 3/4 and 4/4. For that reason, unusual time signatures are normally only used in "serious" music and in jazz, which at this late date is—for the most part—not dance music. Many good examples of the use of "off" time signatures can be found on Dave Brubeck's *Time Out* and *Countdown: Time In Outer Space* albums, and on the Mahavishnu Orchestra's (John McLaughlin's) *Inner Mounting Flame* album, with "The Dance of Maya" (introductory and concluding sections in 10/4, and the bluesy middle section in 20/8) being a particularly entertaining example.

The use of compound meters (time signatures) can also be a fruitful area of exploration. Compound meters have two or three numbers (rather than one) at the top of their time signatures, with a normal single number (usually 4 or 8) on the bottom. Compound signatures are used because the numbers in them accurately reflect the rhythmic patterns in the piece in which they're used. Here are two examples of compound signatures:

Example 106

$$\frac{2+3}{4} \quad \text{rather than} \quad \frac{5}{4} \qquad \frac{3+2+2}{8} \quad \text{rather than} \quad \frac{7}{8}$$

The final "Dance in Bulgarian Rhythm" in Book VI of Bartok's *Mikrokosmos* piano series is an outstanding example of a piece in a complex meter. It's in 3+3+2/8, and it's a very hard driving piece with an almost rock and roll feel, despite its unusual meter.

Breaking up common rhythmic patterns into unusual formations is also an effective means of getting a distinctive sound. A good example of this is "Blue Rondo a la Turk," by Dave Brubeck, in which, much of the time, he breaks up 9/8 (which is normally played with the notes broken up into three groups of three eighth notes, with accents on the first note in all three groups) into three groups of two eighth notes and one group of three eighth notes (with accents on the first note in each group).

7

Instrumentation

This book is intended primarily for solo performers and performers in small groups. Such musicians are usually thoroughly familiar with the abilities and limitations of their own instrument(s) and with those of their fellow performers, if any. They usually have limited access to players of other instruments, and, even if they do, often have no desire to use those players/instruments in their own music. For these reasons, as well as space considerations, a full-blown discussion of instrumentation is outside the scope of this book. Instead, the treatment here will be limited to listing instrumental ranges, characteristics, and transposition ratios.

Range

Authorities differ as to maximum usable instrument ranges; ranges on many instruments will vary from player to player; and in some cases (guitar, for example) ranges will vary from instrument to instrument. So, don't regard the limits given in the following table as absolutes.

If you have access to players you want to use, ask them about their ranges and other technical matters *before* you begin to write. If you're writing without having specific players in mind, it's best to be conservative in terms of instrumental demands unless you're sure that you'll have access to top-notch players when it's time to perform your piece.

Instrumental Ranges

Transposition

Parts for some instruments are customarily written in a different key (or octave) than that in which they're actually played. For example, a written middle C for a B♭ trumpet sounds as the B♭ below middle C. This process is called *transposition*.

In the following table, written notes are represented by whole notes. The notes which would actually sound are represented by quarter notes.

Table 8 (Transposition Ratios)

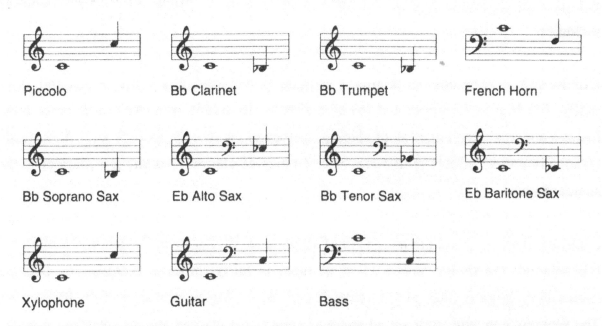

In addition to thinking in terms of notes, it's also helpful to think in terms of keys when dealing with transposing instruments. For instance, if you were writing a piece in the key of F major and you used a B♭ trumpet and a French horn, the trumpet part would be written in the key of G and the horn part in the key of C.

Characteristics

There are dozens upon dozens of orchestral and nonorchestral instruments. For reasons mentioned previously, it's impossible to deal with all, or even most, of them here. Instead, a short discussion of the most useful instruments for rock and jazz groups follows.

Woodwinds

FLUTE — The flute is both agile and versatile. It's very good at playing runs and skips, and it's useful for playing melodies, for improvising, and for doubling instrumental or vocal melodies.

OBOE — The oboe is sluggish compared with the flute and is primarily of use in playing slow and medium-tempo melodies. It's well suited for that task, because it tends to stand out. Due to its reedy quality, the oboe is often used to produce "oriental"-sounding melodies.

CLARINET — The clarinet is almost as agile as the flute, and it plays runs and skips easily. It's best in its upper and lower registers—its middle register is relatively lack-luster—and it's very adept at producing crescendo (gradually louder) and diminuendo (gradually softer) effects. There are several types of clarinet, but the B♭ clarinet is the standard one.

SAXOPHONE — There are four types of saxophone: E♭ baritone; B♭ tenor; E♭ alto; and B♭ soprano; the timbre (tone) of all of them is fairly uniform, though they become successively brighter (though not tremendously so) the higher the range of the instrument. The soprano, alto, and tenor are all about as agile as the clarinet and are excellent melodic and solo instruments. The baritone sax is comparatively sluggish, and is not common in groups without a full saxophone section. Soprano saxes are not all that common, so don't write a part for one unless you're sure that you can come up with one.

Brass

TRUMPET — Two varieties of trumpet are in common use: the B♭, which sounds a major second lower than written, and the C, which sounds as written. The B♭ trumpet is normally used in jazz and other types of popular music. Even though it's often thought of as a fanfare instrument, the trumpet does well with melodies and solos. Several types of mutes are available, all of which greatly diminish the trumpet's loudness.

Some of the more common mutes are:

1) Straight mute—brings out upper overtones; sounds silvery, wispish

2) Harmon mute—squawky, wah-wah effect possible at low volume

3) Wispa mute—similar to Harmon, but quieter

4) Cup mute—dark sounding, cuts down upper overtones

CORNET — The cornet is exactly the same as the B♭ trumpet except that it has a larger mouthpiece and a more graduated bore, which cause it to sound mellower than the trumpet.

FRENCH HORN — The French horn, often referred to simply as the horn, is relatively sluggish, but is well fitted to playing slow and medium-tempo melodies as well as long notes in background figures. Its upper notes (above A or so) are difficult to play and should be avoided in written parts unless you have a very capable player available.

TROMBONE — The articulation of the trombone is very sluggish. Because of this, it's primarily useful for playing long notes in background figures. One attractive feature of the trombone is that it easily produces a useful special effect: the *glissando*, or slide. The trombone is about as powerful as the trumpet, and the same types of mutes can be used with it as with the trumpet.

Strings

VIOLIN — The violin is extremely versatile. It's ideal for playing melodies and solos, but is also at home playing background figures and harmonies. (But be careful—in jazz, rock, sleazy listening, etc., background strings often sound disgustingly syrupy.) Though not well suited to playing rapid wide skips, the violin is adept at playing runs and arpeggios, and can produce a wide range of special effects. Among the most popular are *tremolo* (indicated with three short lines through the note stem[s]); *glissando* (indicated "gliss," or with a wavy line connecting the beginning and ending notes); *pizzicato* (plucked—indicated "pizz"); and harmonic notes, which sound glassy, flute-like. One way to indicate harmonics is to write an open, diamond-shaped notehead a perfect 4th above any desired note; the resultant harmonic will sound two octaves above the lower written note (which will not sound). Harmonic notes of this type are called *artificial* harmonics.

Example 106

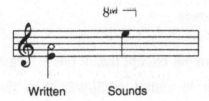

Written   Sounds

Another type, *natural* harmonics, are also easy to produce—but only at a few places on the violin's neck. (These correspond to the places where you can produce bell notes on a guitar's neck.) You can indicate natural harmonics by placing a small circle above a note head. The following example shows where natural harmonics can be produced on a violin's G string.

Example 107

Written

Natural harmonics can be produced on the other strings at the corresponding places on the neck. For example, natural harmonics can be produced on the D string exactly a fifth above the harmonics produced on the G string. The natural harmonics on the A string will be a fifth above those on the D string; and the natural harmonics on the E string will be a fifth above those on the A string. (The violin has four strings tuned in perfect fifths, the G string being the lowest.)

VIOLA — The viola is very similar to the violin, but is slightly larger, sounds a fifth lower, and is a bit rougher in tone.

CELLO — The cello is much larger and less agile than the violin and viola, but it still does well playing melodies in its upper register as well as bass lines in its lower register.

BASS — The acoustic bass is awkward compared with the other strings. Its only use in popular music is as the bass instrument in some jazz and bluegrass groups; when used in that capacity, it's almost always played pizzicato (plucked).

Nonorchestral Instruments

XYLOPHONE — The xylophone is a keyboard percussion instrument. It sounds high, dry, and brittle, and is well suited to playing arpeggios, glissandos, and rapid repeated notes and patterns.

MARIMBA — The marimba is similar to the xylophone, but its range is lower in pitch and it has a much mellower tone, which makes it more suited to playing melodies than the xylophone.

VIBRAPHONE — The vibraphone is basically a metal marimba. It has a very mellow, bell-like tone, which makes it a good choice for playing melodies and solos. Because it can sustain notes virtually forever, it's well suited to playing background harmonies. But don't write chords for it containing more than four notes—like all keyboard percussion instruments, the vibraphone is played with mallets, and two mallets per hand is the maximum.

GUITAR — Guitars come in a great variety of types, but all are well suited to playing runs, chords, background figures, and relatively narrow leaps (two-and-a-half octaves at most, leaps of an octave or less being the easiest to make). All guitars are also capable of a wide variety of special effects including glissandos, bell notes, and bent notes.

BASS GUITAR — The electric bass is much less agile than the electric guitar, and is suited only to playing one-note-at-a-time bass lines. Its tone can range from muddy to very crisp depending on the player and tone settings. Like the guitar, it can produce glissandos and bell notes. (Bent notes are possible, but rarely used on the electric bass.)

Bibliography

Compositional Techniques

Cope, David. *New Music Composition*. New York: Schirmer Books, 1977. (a gold mine of information on pointillism, tone color melody, rows, clusters, and much more)

Dallin, Leon. *Techniques of Twentieth Century Composition*. Madison, Wisc.: Brown & Benchmark, 1974.

Risatti, Howard. *New Music Vocabulary*. Urbana, Illinois: University of Illinois Press, 1976. (an encyclopedia of avant-garde techniques and notation)

Russo, William. *Composing Music: A New Approach*. Chicago: University of Chicago Press, 1988.

Counterpoint

Jeppesen, Knud. *Counterpoint*. Englewood Cliffs, N.J.: Prentice-Hall, 1939. (16th century counterpoint)

Kennan, Kent. *Counterpoint*. Englewood Cliffs, N.J.: Prentice-Hall, 1959. (18th century counterpoint)

Lytle, Victor. *The Theory and Practice of Strict Counterpoint*. Philadelphia: Oliver Ditson Co., 1939. (16th century counterpoint)

Piston, Walter. *Counterpoint*. New York: WW. Norton & Co., 1947. (18th century counterpoint)

Form

Adair, Audrey. *Types of Musical Form & Composition*. Englewood Cliffs, N.J.: Prentice-Hall, 1987.

Coker, Jerry. *Improvising Jazz*. Englewood Cliffs, N.J.: Prentice-Hall, 1964. (blues & jazz forms)

Hodson, Geoffrey. *Music Forms*. Wheaton, Illinois: Theosophical Publishing House, 1987.

Tyndall, Robert. *Musical Form*. Westport, Connecticut: Greenwood Press, 1977.

Harmony

Persichetti, Vincent. *Twentieth Century Harmony*. New York: W.W. Norton & Co., 1961. (filled with interesting ideas and useful information)

Piston, Walter. *Harmony*. New York: W.W. Norton & Co., 1969. (*the* standard academic harmony text)

Schoenberg, Arnold. *Structural Functions of Harmony*. New York: W.W. Norton & Co., 1964.

Instrumentation

Brindle, Reginald Smith. *Contemporary Percussion*. New York: Oxford University Press, 1975. (the best single work on percussion)

Forsyth, Cecil. *Orchestration*. New York: Macmillan, 1946.

Kennan, Kent. *The Technique of Orchestration*. Englewood Cliffs, N.J.: Prentice-Hall, 1983.

Lorrin, Mark. *Dictionary of Bowing and Tonal Techniques for Strings*. Miami Beach: Folk World, 1968.

McKay, George. *Creative Orchestration*. Boston: Allyn & Bacon, 1963. (short, contains good information on the relationship of composition and orchestration)

Palmer, King. *Orchestration*. London: St. Paul's House, 1973. (short, easy to understand)

Reed, H. Owen and Leach, Joel. *Scoring for Percussion*. (good for those unfamiliar with percussion)

Rimsky-Korsakov, Nikolay. *Principles of Orchestration*. New York: Dover, 1964.

Jazz

Coker, Jerry. *Improvising Jazz*. Englewood Cliffs, N.J.: Prentice-Hall, 1964.
The Jazz Idiom. Englewood Cliffs, N.J.: Prentice-Hall, 1975.

Russo, William. *Composing for the Jazz Orchestra*. Chicago: University of Chicago Press, 1961.

Melody

Coker, Jerry. *Improvising Jazz*. Englewood Cliffs, N.J.: Prentice-Hall, 1964. (useful info on soloing)

Kennan, Kent. *Counterpoint*. Englewood Cliffs, N.J.: Prentice-Hall, 1959. (good general info on melodies)